Ugomma the Notorious Mistress

A true short story

Joseph C. Amadi

authorHOUSE®

AuthorHouse™ UK Ltd.
500 Avebury Boulevard
Central Milton Keynes, MK9 2BE
www.authorhouse.co.uk
Phone: 08001974150

First published by AuthorHouse 05/06/2011

ISBN: 978-1-4567-7844-6 (sc)
ISBN: 978-1-4567-7845-3 (ebk)

To my family

Prologue

Ugomma (aka Mamiwater, which literally means Mother of Oceans) was an evil, heartless and callous woman, who became extremely notorious in the 1980s. She was very popular with numerous male friends, and was well known in the area.

Ugomma lived a lavish lifestyle and was often seen in the company of the rich and famous. She was a very clever and attractive woman, who always remained confident that in the future she would become a super glamour model. She deliberately targeted wealthy and prominent people, not just for her own sexual gratification or for financial interest, but specifically to raise her profile. As a result of her intimate relationships with many men, most women around her area saw Ugomma, not only as a potential threat, but also as a husband snatcher.

Ugomma was an only daughter who grew up in a devout Christian family. She was ostracised when she was disowned by her father, and was verbally abused, shamed, disgraced and embarrassed on several occasions. She was physically assaulted by the wife of one of her lovers, who claimed she had entered into an affair with her husband, and Ugomma suffered horrific injuries.

Most importantly, Ugomma was a well-educated intelligent woman; a woman with a highly competitive spirit. She was married twice, both her husbands being polygamous. Her first marriage to Chief Ibeneme lasted barely a year. After, she was accused by her ex-husband of being infertile, incapable of bearing children. A few years later after her divorce, she met Chief Obi, whom she married, but after few months she found herself in a vulnerable position, tragically caught up in a ritual murder orchestrated by her so-called husband, to whom she devoted her life with love and trust.

One

Ugomma was born in Ghana to a Nigerian father and Ghanaian mother, the only daughter of Chief and Lolo Vincent Onyeme. She moved to Nigeria at an early age. She was educated at top Nigerian schools and graduated in law. She came from a wealthy family in Umuowa community in Imo-state.

Ugomma's father, Chief Onyeme, was a very wealthy and highly respected man. He was made a local paramount Chief of Umuowa. Two years later he became the traditional ruler of Umuowa community. Ugomma's parents were well known for being a compassionate, humble and helpful couple. In addition, Chief Onyeme, an oil magnate, was regarded by his community as being the godfather of Umuowa and a philanthropist. Ugomma's father had contributed immensely to his community, and also neighbouring communities in Imo-state and Abia-state. He built a stylish and contemporary multi-purpose town hall, brought electricity to the community, sunk a borehole for water and organised free medical health care. Additionally, Chief Onyeme made over ten million naira available to peasant farmers in Umuowa, as well as scholarships for sons and daughters of Umuowa, Umuokoro and Eluoha, which had been almost non-existent for some time in Umuowa, but was now widespread. Chief Onyeme was a very talented man. He was formally educated both in Ghana and Nigeria. He was also a legal practitioner with over thirty-five years' experience in the legal profession.

Ugomma's mother, Lolo Christina (nee Egoyibo), was a devout Christian, well educated, exuberant and a woman of impeccable character. She was the one who had a great influence on Ugomma's upbringing, encouraging and advising her daughter to fulfil her true potential. Christina also played a vital role in assisting her daughter, Ugomma, in her professional aspiration. She and her husband warned their daughter to desist from indulging in any sexual activities with married men, but Ugomma ignored her parents' advice. Her parents went on to remind Ugomma of some of the unknown circumstances that are experienced in a polygamous home.

"Ugomma, our daughter, are you fully aware that we expect you to be a good role model? Why can't you make use of your simple initiative by trying to find a decent and responsible future partner, instead of hanging around with sugar daddies? If you don't stay away from this immoral way of life, you will ruin your good reputation!"

* * *

Ignoring her parents' warning, Ugomma went on to marry Chief Ibeneme, whom she had met years before

2

during her legal service course. However, Chief Ibeneme, a gynaecologist, ran a medical practice in Port Harcourt and was still in a good relationship with his first wife, Oby. He ignored his wife's early warning about taking Ugomma as his second wife. Consequently, five months after the marriage to Ugomma, things started to turn from bad to worse. Apparently, both couples started to accuse each other of all sorts of stupid things. Chief Ibeneme accused his wife, Ugomma, of being incapable of bearing children, unfaithful, arrogant and a selfish woman.

"I made a dreadful mistake in marrying Ugomma," he admitted. He expected Ugomma to tend the house, and to show him obedience and respect. "If a man perceives that his wife has somehow failed in her role, stepped beyond her boundaries or challenged him, then he is within his rights to react violently," he said. He also added, "It is true that girls from wealthy families get spoilt and take advantage of their parents' wealth."

Ugomma wasn't obeying him, never had food ready on time, and had no clue about household chores like cooking and washing-up, always leaving the entire domestic jobs for the poor little housemaid. Furthermore, she questioned him about his money all the time. He described her as being uncivil, uncultured, and that her behaviour was completely unacceptable.

Ugomma accused her husband, Chief Ibeneme, of being a bully, also that he was impotent and unable to fulfil his marital obligation towards her. She further criticised her husband's manhood, by comparing it to that of a little boy. Ugomma disclosed that:

3

"Going somewhere without his permission turns out to be a huge calamity in our house."

A few weeks later as the turmoil continued, both husband and wife were caught engaging in a shameful street fight along Ikwerre Road in Port Harcourt, after Ugomma revealed that she was having an affair with one of his close family friends, who had come to stay with them for just one week. As a result, Ugomma was brutally beaten by her husband after she failed to offer a genuine explanation as to why she had slept with her husband's family friend. Consequently, she was absolutely shocked, terrified and devastated after she found herself with a broken nose and a broken jaw, sustained from her husband.

Barely a week after her conflict with her husband, Chief Ibeneme, Ugomma was involved in another confrontation with her husband's first wife, Oby. Ugomma was spotted exchanging blows with Oby in one of the Total petrol stations in Port Harcourt. Both women had been on their way to the Sunday service, accompanied by their husband's private chauffeur, who was driving them to the nearby church. However, it was a premeditated attack planned by Oby due to being unfairly treated by her husband since the arrival of Ugomma.

"Since Ugomma came into this house as the second wife of my husband, my rights have been taken away from me," she said.

She had been deprived of so many things in the house that she no longer received full attention from her husband, pocket money to look after herself or the usual gifts from her husband. She was at that moment struggling to make end meet, so her plan was to find an opportunity to either get rid of Ugomma or to eliminate her from the vicinity. She would then recover the full control of the house, which had been taken over by Ugomma.

Ugomma was in floods of tears, worried and tense, as she was repeatedly beaten by Oby and almost stripped bare, but thanks to her family driver, she was rescued from her husband's first wife's cruelty.

After her battle with Oby, Ugomma was again involved in another sexual perversion scandal with her brother-in-law. Ugomma was caught having sex with Oga Mike in the famous Takwabe Hotel situated about one hundred and twenty yards from the Ndiowu village. However, the incident came to light after a tip-off from the hotel's female waitress who knew Ugomma's husband. Shortly after, he arrived and didn't waste any time in beating and punching both Ugomma and Oga Mike, both of whom were left with bruises, scars and bleeding noses.

Chief Ibeneme, who had earlier described his wife Ugomma as the worst woman ever seen stated:

"I am to blame because I rushed into marriage with Ugomma without knowing her well. It was my mistake. As far as I am concerned, Ugomma, my wife, will soon be removed or sent back to her parents, and she should know by now that her relationship with me has ended. The law of this land, Ndiowu community, forbids abomination, and as a result whoever commits such a despicable crime should face severe physical punishment and expulsion."

Soon after, Chief Ibeneme took all his compelling evidence against his wife Ugomma and his brother Oga Mike to the elders, who would decide what would follow next. The town crier (or bell man) of the Ndiowu natives was immediately sent out by the elders to announce they expected everyone to assemble at the Umuadi market square as soon as possible.

* * *

A few hours later, when everyone had gathered together at the market square, Chief Ibeneme was the first person to be called upon to explain to the elders what had actually happened, and how he was informed of the situation.

"Since I married my wife, Ugomma, she has been cheating on me, not once, but several times. A few months ago she had an affair with my close best friend, but I decided not to inform the elders. Besides this, which is bad enough, Ugomma has engaged in shameful street fights with me and my first wife, Oby. All I want now is that Ugomma has to be shamed and she should receive her rightful physical punishment as well as being returned to her parental home. She has brought shame to me, my family and the entire Ndiowu natives' town. Since both my brother and Ugomma have committed abomination, I would like my brother, Oga Mike, to face his own physical punishment and be expelled from our land."

The next person to be called or summoned to testify before the elders was the hotel's female waitress, who went on to explain how Ugomma and Oga Mike had come to check into one of the rooms in the hotel, and how long both spent there before they were apprehended by Chief Ibeneme after the tip-off.

Soon after, Igwe, the head of the tribe, immediately ordered all the women present at the market square, the venue of the trial, to go and get Ugomma and Oga Mike. They both appeared before the elders with their hands tied behind their backs. Ugomma looked haggard and exhausted, and both appeared to be quite apprehensive while waiting to hear their fate from the elders. Igwe began by explaining to them the gravity of the offence they had both committed, and the law that applied to it. He went on further to disclose to them the current laws of the community in Ndiowu.

"Anyone who breaches any of the laws in our Ndiowu community could face either severe physical punishment or immediate expulsion," he explained. "I have heard individual opinions from both the elders and others present at the market square, on what punishment should be recommended for both of you."

After a few minutes it was unanimously decided that mandatory whipping and immediate expulsion was the punishment for Ugomma and Oga Mike. Soon after, both were dragged to the outskirts of Ndiowu, where they were stripped of their clothes before being subjected to a prolonged beating - twenty-four lashes of a cane on their bare butts.

Ugomma lifted her hands to the heavens as she continually cried, while the Ndiowu women were dancing, singing and chanting her name, 'Ugomma Olala Olala', meaning that Ugomma was heading for her parents' home. After the caning, Ugomma was barred from returning to Ndiowu town indefinitely, and was eventually handed over to her parents with nothing and without sympathy. In addition, she was ordered to reimburse her husband, Chief Ibeneme, for the expenditure she had incurred. Her accomplice, Oga Mike, was banned from returning for forty-eight hours.

In apparent retaliation by her parents for the embarrassment, shame and disgrace their only daughter had brought upon their family, they disowned her. She was also denied all entitlements and benefits, including physical cash and properties that she would have inherited from her parents. Ugomma suffered another setback when she was finally evicted from her parents' home. In addition, she lost contact with them and was not on speaking terms with anyone, including her immediate family.

Ugomma remained incommunicado after she was evicted by her parents, and no one knew her whereabouts until she married her second husband, Chief Obi.

Two

Two years after her first marriage to Chief Ibeneme ended, Ugomma met Chief Obi when she had given up all hope. She couldn't hold back her feelings - it was like a dream come true. She never felt shy or embarrassed on that memorable day.

Chief Obi was charmed with Ugomma's beauty and humility, and vowed never to leave her. He was a polygamist, married to two women and had six children. He was famous, highly respected, very wealthy and a local paramount Chief in Umuokoro, his community. He was a very devoted Christian, a philanthropist and a member of many social clubs as well as secret societies.

Speculation and rumours started to spread that Chief Obi had constantly been seen with Ugomma. One Saturday evening, Ugomma and Chief Obi were enjoying themselves at the famous and expensive Green Garden Hotel at Okpe Junction. As both were drinking - no one knows how, only God knows - Chief Obi's second wife, Ijeoma, managed to trace Chief Obi to their usual rendezvous. It was suggested that it might have been as a result of a tip-off; it was highly likely an informant, who knew Chief Obi's wives, had alerted Ijeoma, which was very prevalent in the area.

Ugomma was devastated, shocked and couldn't believe what was happening when Ijeoma took them by surprise. Ugomma was assaulted; beaten up, her clothes and underwear torn to shreds. She was nearly strangled, humiliated, shamed and verbally threatened by Chief Obi's wife. Ugomma was given the disgrace of her life as she ran out of the hotel with hardly anything covering her bare body. In addition, she was not given the opportunity to retrieve her shoes and she didn't remember to take her purse or even food from the meal on the table.

* * *

A few months later, after the conflict with Ijeoma, Chief Obi's wife, Ugomma was contacted by her lover, Chief Obi, who had fled from the hotel vicinity when the fight broke out. Ugomma couldn't hold back her feelings, as she never thought she would be reunited with him again. Soon after, she left for Chief Obi's home to honour her invitation.

When she arrived at Chief Obi's compound, while he was away, Ugomma was met by Ijeoma and Ify, who refused her entry into the house. She was disgraced, embarrassed and verbally abused, and to add insult to injury, they spat in her face. Later on, both women claimed that her visit to Chief Obi's house was uncalled for, so realising it was almost impossible to gain access to Chief Obi's house, Ugomma decided to depart.

As she was making her way back home, she was fortunate to be met by Chief Obi on his return from his office. He apologised immediately, and she driven back to his house. Soon after she arrived at the house, Ijeoma and Ify were warned to desist from tormenting Ugomma or both would face the consequences. Both wives were devastated by their husband's warning and they described his behaviour as unacceptable. Meanwhile, Ugomma who faced a hostile reception from Ijeoma and Ify, knew quite well that there would be more problems, conflicts and dangers ahead.

* * *

Some time later Ugomma had fully moved into Chief Obi's house and settled down as his third wife. She became an outcast, enemy and the black sheep of the family. Ijeoma and Ify became jealous and envious of her, and she was ignored by both women.

Ugomma became a complete housemaid, but whatever she did in the house was wrong. After a while, both Chief Obi and his two wives turned against Ugomma, all three refusing to talk to her or eat the food she had prepared. At a later stage when her situation in Chief Obi's house became unbearable, despite stiff opposition from both wives, she chose to remain silent because she has no other place to go.

She was having a difficult time coming to terms with what had happened to her. She was also experiencing negative emotions - self-blame and anger. She described her feelings to her husband, Chief Obi. She spoke of his devastating act of betrayal because someone she had trusted, married, loved and with whom she shared things in common, and someone who had brought her into his house had later plotted, along with two of his wives, to turn against her for no reason. She further added it was a complete disaster, and demanded to know what had gone wrong with her husband, but was denied an answer. In the situation she found herself there wasn't much she could do about it, but Ugomma recalled her parents' early warning.

"My parents predicted my romance with polygamist, Chief Obi, could ruin me."

* * *

Ten weeks later, after realising her relationship with her husband, along with two of his wives, had become menacing, she became quite apprehensive, thinking an imminent attack was inevitable.

One week later, her mutilated body was found dumped in the bush with some of her body parts missing. She was discovered just a few miles away from her matrimonial home.

Soon after, her husband, Chief Obi, was interviewed in connection with her death, but claimed that he knew nothing about it. Love rat, Chief Obi, who had previously denied any involvement or act of conspiracy to murder his wife Ugomma, during police interrogation, claimed responsibility for his wife's brutal murder after human body parts, one empty coffin and two deadly weapons were discovered when the police raided his shrine.

Three

One month after Ugomma's death and while her dead body was still in the mortuary in the nearby hospital in Umuokoro town, Ugomma's father, Chief Vincent Onyeme, heard the news of his daughter's untimely tragic death and reacted angrily, as it had come as a dreadful shock to him. Despite the fact that he had lost contact with her, had not even been on speaking terms with his daughter and had no knowledge about her marriage to Chief Obi, he found the courage to summon his elders to discuss his daughter's death as well as her forthcoming funeral ceremony.

As they all gathered at his compound in Umuowa town, Ugomma's father, Chief Vincent Onyeme, began to address his elders.

"How on earth can my only daughter, Ugomma, be left to be buried by a person who has not even paid her dowry? Besides, her so-called husband, Chief Obi, stole my daughter, and was definitely responsible for her death. It is a complete abomination to allow my daughter to be buried in a town where her bride price has not been settled." He shook his head. "No way. We are going to do everything we can to retrieve Ugomma's body from Umuokoro town and bury her in my compound."

Soon after his speech, the Igwe Ezenwa, the head of the elders, began to speak. "Irrespective of whatever happened between our late sister, Ugomma, and us, whatever she did to us or the shame she brought to this town Umuowa, despite all that she is still our dear beloved sister. For this obvious reason, we are going to fight tooth and nail, and thereby redouble our efforts to retrieve our sister's dead body from the stronghold of Umuokoro town as soon as possible, if they fail to meet the demands we are going to make available to them," he said. "Hence, Chief Obi, who took our sister for quite a long period of time without paying for her bride price, will be forced to either marry dead Ugomma or pay for her dowry, thereby retaining full ownership of Ugomma as his wife, or he will face the serious consequences. He has violated the law of our land, Umuowa, by taking our sister from her parents' home without settling for her bride price. As a result, Ugomma was killed by him, therefore, if we fail to act now it will further damage our reputation." The Igwe Ezenwa, further added, "To the detriment of Umuowa town, the only way we can restore our reputation, dignity and respect is to revolt against Chief Obi and his people."

* * *

The next day they all left to retrieve Ugomma's body from Umuokoro town. Her mother, Lolo Christina, who was devastated by her daughter's death, had earlier informed her husband, Chief Onyeme, that she really did not wish to travel along with her husband and the elders to repatriate Ugomma's body back from Umuokoro town. However, as they were just a few miles away approaching Umuokoro town, Lolo Christina collapsed and became unconscious. A few minutes later she was pronounced dead as they were trying to resuscitate her. The planned trip did not go ahead, it was called off. Her body was immediately flown back to Umuowa town, where she was taken to the mortuary until further notice.

Ugomma's father, still in a state of shock, shed tears for his lost wife. He described his wife's death as a terrible nightmare, a huge loss and a double tragedy.

"This is another setback, but, as a result, the struggle must continue. We must never give up in our fight to retrieve my daughter's body from her husband's hometown of Umuokoro," he said. "I pay tribute to my wife, a truly magnificent woman, who sacrificed so much and gave up her life for her daughter, Ugomma."

The Igwe Ezenwa, who was accompanying the elders when Ugomma's mother collapsed, began by paying tribute to Ugomma's father, Chief Onyeme.

"We are absolutely shocked by what has happened. Firstly our heart goes out to Chief Onyeme and his family, but more crucially, our mission to retrieve Ugomma's body from her husband's place must be accomplished. We must never be frightened by the Umuokoro town elders, irrespective of these unforeseen circumstances. We will soon be embarking on our journey to Umuokoro town."

* * *

One week after Lolo Christina's death, Ugomma's father and his elders journeyed for the second time to retrieve Ugomma's dead body from her husband's hometown of Umuokoro. However, on their arrival they were met by a large crowd that had gathered to pay their last respects outside Chief Obi's compound. Moreover, they were singing, dancing and praying whilst waiting for Ugomma's burial time, which was scheduled for that very day, being the Orie Amaraku day.

Chief Onyeme and his elders took them by surprise. As they were unaware of any such arrangements for the burial they immediately asked for both Ugomma's husband and his elders to come forward for an urgent discussion regarding Ugomma's bride price and her burial ceremony. As they all sat down in front of Chief Obi's house, the Igwe Ezenwa began to explain to Chief Obi and his elders the reasons behind their visit.

"Chief Obi, we think you should be informed as to why we have visited your house today. We are here to let you know that you have violated our law and, as a result, you could be facing the consequences. Chief Obi, you kidnapped Ugomma and was living with her until her death, with neither her parents' consent nor her bride price being paid. You were responsible for Ugomma's death, and now you want her to be buried in your hometown Umuokoro without any of the above listed conditions being met." He shook his head twice. "God forbid that."

He told Chief Obi that he was to settle Ugomma's bride price and go ahead with her planned burial ceremony in his hometown or Ugomma's body would be flown back to her parents' hometown Umuowa, for a befitting burial.

Soon after the Igwe Ezenwa's speech, Ugomma's husband, Chief Obi, and his elders replied:

"No way, we don't agree."

It was then that the head of the Umuokoro elders insisted that:

"This was a terrible tragedy, the like of which has never happened in this town before. Ugomma was disowned by her father, Chief Onyeme, and, as a result, they were still not on speaking terms when she died. In addition, she lost contact with the other members of her immediate family and because of that it was absolutely impossible for Ugomma's husband to contact his father in-law. Ugomma was living with Chief Obi until her death, despite the fact that her dowry had not been paid or settled. It is against our tradition to allow her body to be taken away from our town Umuokoro. Ugomma must be buried in this town according to our tradition, but if the Umuowa elders refuse to accept this then we must engage in war with them," he concluded.

Half an hour later, as Ugomma's husband, Chief Obi, and his elders had refused to accept the conditions given to them by Umuowa's elders, Ugomma's body was immediately brought out from her husband's house and taken to the ambulance car waiting to transport her back to Umuowa.

* * *

Fighting soon broke out between the two neighbouring towns of Umuowa and Umuokoro.

Ugomma's father, Chief Onyeme, was shot by Umuokoro village vigilante men and was immediately taken to the nearby hospital. One hour later, after an operation to remove the bullets from his body, he was pronounced dead. As a result, his body was taken to the mortuary where his wife's body had been resting to be buried at a later date.

Shortly after Ugomma's father's tragic death, the Igwe of Umuowa town, Igwe Ezenwa, addressed his elders.

"It was not long ago that we lost Chief Onyeme's wife, and today we have also lost Chief Onyeme in a dreadful shooting. My people, don't forget that God gives life and it is He who takes it away. Most importantly, Ugomma's body has finally been retrieved from her husband's hometown Umuokoro."

Shortly after his speech, Igwe Ezenwa pronounced the burial date for both Ugomma and her parents.

Muguette Goufrani

Four

Seven months after Ugomma and her parents' death, Chief Obi started to face one problem after another. The situation seemed to become steadily worse - day by day and week by week - until he was absolutely obsessed with thoughts of the recent happenings. At night he was unable to sleep alone in his own bedroom, and not one of his two wives was willing or eager to sleep with him there.

Chief Obi decided to vacate his bedroom so that Ugomma's spirit would no longer disturb him. She had been trying to appear in his dreams and he proclaimed seeing her spirit whenever he went to bed at night. One week later, Chief Obi began to wonder what had gone wrong, and why he was still seeing Ugomma almost every night.

"What should I do now?" he asked. "Should I consult the voodoo man (native debia) first and try to find out what is wrong, or shall I go ahead and inform the elders of Umuokoro town, who might have a solution and thereby advise me about what to do next to rectify this problem? My mind needs to be at rest."

As Chief Obi was contemplating what to do to solve his ongoing problem, his two wives arrived, so he explained what he intended to do about his sleeplessness nights. Immediately both wives, Ijeoma and Ify, burst out laughing and whooped at their husband.

"Our husband, Chief Obi, are you out of your mind?" Ify enquired.

"Have you forgotten that you were the person responsible for Ugomma's death?" asked Ijeoma.

"Why are you complaining? Anyway, we hope this is just the beginning of your problems. We believe you should expect more to come."

"Our husband, Chief Obi, we believe whatever retribution given to you is justified."

Both women further warned their husband, Chief Obi, by saying:

"Have you spoken to anyone else about your ongoing problem?"

"No!" Chief Obi exclaimed.

They told Chief Obi that he must never tell any person about his so-called sleeplessness night star, or they would expose him to the end.

"We all know what you did to Ugomma before her death, but we have decided to remain silent in order to protect you from Ugomma's parents and the elders. If you fail to accept our instructions given to you right now, you will be inviting your own early grave, OK? Whatever happens to you, you must never mention our names."

Ijeoma and Ify were afraid that their husband, Chief Obi, might reveal their secret to his elders on how the three of them conspired to murder Ugomma, as he was deliberating over what to do to end his ongoing insomnia.

* * *

One evening a week later, after dinner, which had been cooked by his two wives, Chief Obi collapsed within an hour of eating his meal. He was vomiting blood, so was immediately rushed to the hospital by his two wives.

Two days later his condition had deteriorated and, as a result of his constant vomiting, pain and internal bleeding, he was placed in the intensive care unit whilst the doctor was busily trying to establish the reason for the extent of the food poisoning. On completion of the tests the doctor updated Chief Obi's family and other members of his immediate circle, who were waiting anxiously to obtain information about Chief Obi's condition.

"Based on the medical tests carried out on Chief Obi," the doctor informed them, "I confirm that he was poisoned with food. At the moment Chief Obi has been placed in the intensive care unit. He is in a very critical condition, in deep pain, and I have to inform you that Chief Obi may not survive. Let us all cross our fingers."

Both wives, Ijeoma and Ify, burst into tears.

"Chimoo, who did this to our lovely husband, and who will look after us and the children now?" sobbed Ify.

"God, why did you allow our husband, Chief Obi, to be taken away from us?" wailed Ijeoma.

They told all those present that when the head of the household dies, the house becomes an empty shell. As both wives were suggesting who might be behind their husband's food poisoning, news came from the hospital that Chief Obi had passed away.

The news came as a shock, as both wives and the Umuokoro elders could not believe what had transpired. The entire Umuokoro community was absolutely silent, because Chief Obi was regarded as the pillar and godfather of his town, Umuokoro. He was also the man behind the development of his town, Umuokoro. He was seen as an important figure, not only in his own town, but also other neighbouring communities.

* * *

One hour after the news of Chief Obi's death was announced, the head of the Umuokoro community, the Igwe, immediately called an emergency meeting summoning all their sons and daughters, both young and old, to his royal palace. As they all gathered at the Igwe's palace, he spoke to those assembled there.

"Ijeoma and Ify, please, I want to hear from you both if you are responsible for your husband's sudden death. According to the autopsy report disclosed by the chief medical practitioner, Chief Obi died as a result of food poisoning. We are so devastated by Chief Obi's murder, and we will do everything we can to find the perpetrator of this dreadful deed. Ijeoma and Ify, which of you gave the poisoned food to your husband, Chief Obi? I am asking both of you for the second time, but still there is no sign of any confession."

Ijeoma and Ify both emphatically denied poisoning Chief Obi.

The Igwe continued:

"We no longer believe what the two women say, and since both wives have refused to disclose any information about their husband's death, we will do whatever it takes to apprehend Chief Obi's killer. We will soon be meeting with the native voodoo man (debia) who will assist us in identifying the person or persons behind Chief Obi's food poisoning that killed him - we shall leave no stone unturned."

It was quite obvious that almost every death occurring mostly in African countries was treated as suspicious, even if the person died as a result of an accident or of natural causes. It was the task of the local debia or voodoo man to ascertain who was behind a person's death. He was always regarded as extremely powerful and whatever he said was undisputed and final.

* * *

The fact-finding mission began two hours later. Everyone went to the home of the local voodoo man. The Igwe spoke.

"Nnayi Onye debia, we have come for your help. Our brother, Chief Obi, was poisoned after having his dinner prepared by his two wives, and we do not know who was responsible. We would like to find out through you if our late brother, Chief Obi, was poisoned by his two wives or by our enemies, the Umuowa elders. Please, Nnayi Onye debia, reveal it to us now. Our heart is broken, because our brother, Chief Obi, did not deserve to be poisoned."

Soon after the Igwe's speech, the voodoo man, Chief Onye Egbula Nwanneya, began by saying:

"My people, you are all warmly welcomed. I have heard what you have said, but before I commence my duty I would expect some materials from you to enable me to carry out the job today. If none of these are available now, I would expect to receive some money from you, so that I can send one of my servants to purchase all the listed items as quickly as possible. If you are unable to do this I advise all of you to go home and return with everything I have requested by tomorrow."

The Igwe replied by saying:

"Nnanyi Onye debia, have this money from me and send someone to buy what you need whilst we are waiting. We want to know the outcome by today, which would enable us to execute our actions on both wives as quickly as possible without any further delay. Whoever kills an innocent person must also be killed, and we all believe that Chief Obi was poisoned by his two wives, Ijeoma and Ify. We are all aware that Ijeoma and Ify will receive the tough and harsh capital punishment set aside for them by the native debia as soon as both wives have been confirmed as being behind their husband's death."

A few minutes later the Igwe and his elders, alongside Ijeoma and Ify, were all taken into the cottage by the voodoo man, who consulted his oracles (Juju) and spoke to those assembled there.

"It is confirmed that the late Chief Obi was poisoned by a woman," was all he said, refusing to name any names.

The Igwe, who was quite optimistic and confident that both wives, Ijeoma and Ify, were responsible for their husband's death, was deeply disappointed and miserable after hearing that - not the outcome he had expected - from the native voodoo man. The Igwe described what he had pronounced as absolute nonsense, angrily shaking his head.

"Let us get out of here, this is nothing but a shambles," he said.

Both wives, Ijeoma and Ify, were delighted that the voodoo man had failed to name them as the culprits, as he feared that they could be targeted or killed by the angry Umuokoro elders.

Soon afterwards they were snubbed by the Igwe.

"Egotist and tyrant, Igwe, shame on you and your elders," they said.

Epilogue

Ugomma

On the day of the burial there was a large turnout of Umuowa town natives, both young and old, wearing spectacular traditional costume. The burial rites were given, followed by a one hundred and twenty gun salute, along with many cultural dances and masquerades from Umuowa town, Eluoha community and Ndiowu town.

Ugomma and her parents were buried with Christian rites in the same place in Umuowa town, which shocked the entire Umuowa community. Soon after the funeral ceremony, the Igwe Ezenwa, the head of the elders of Umuowa's autonomous community, paid a great tribute to the late Ugomma's parents, Chief and Lolo Vincent Onyeme.

"There is no smoke without fire. Ugomma and her parents' death was a huge loss. Chief Onyeme and his wife paid the ultimate price as a result of Ugomma's unacceptable behaviour, selfish and immoral acts.

Ugomma and her parents would have been alive today if only she had listened to her parents' advice."

Chief Obi

Ugomma's husband, Chief Obi, died as a result of his own nemesis, but it still remains unclear as to who poisoned him, as no one, even his two wives, Ijeoma and Ify, denied responsibility for his death.

Glossary of Nigerian Terms

Ugomma	-beautiful girl
Mamiwate	-Mother of Oceans
Lolo	-Mrs
Igwe	-traditional ruler
Oga Mike	-Mr Mike
Ola, Olala	-holding back, returning back
Umuebi	-town, community
Umuowa	-town, community
Umuokoro	-town, community
Eluoha	-town, community
Umuadi	-town, community
Ndiowu	-town, community
Obi na etiti	-town
Okpe	-city
Orie Amaraku	-community open market
Nee Egoyibo	-foreign currency
Nnanyi Onye debia	-voodoo man/native doctor
Chimoo	-my God
Debia	- voodoo man/native doctor
Chief Onye Egbula Nwanne	- voodoo man

www.ingramcontent.com/pod-product-compliance
Lightning Source LLC
Chambersburg PA
CBHW050348290526
45785CB00006B/2685